Pebble® Plus

Animal Kingdom Questions and Answers

Insects
A Question and Answer Book

by Isabel Martin

Consulting Editor: Gail Saunders-Smith, PhD

CAPSTONE PRESS
a capstone imprint

Pebble Plus is published by Capstone Press,
1710 Roe Crest Drive, North Mankato, Minnesota 56003
www.capstonepub.com

Library of Congress Cataloging-in-Publication Data
Martin, Isabel, 1977–
    Insects : a question and answer book / by Isabel Martin.
        pages cm. — (Pebble plus. Animal kingdom questions and answers)
    Includes bibliographical references and index.
    Summary: "Simple text and colorful images illustrate types of insects, including common characteristics, diet, and life cycle"—Provided by publisher.
    Audience: Ages 4–8.
    Audience: Grades K–3.
    ISBN 978-1-4914-0564-2 (library binding) — ISBN 978-1-4914-0632-8 (paperback) — ISBN 978-1-4914-0598-7 (eBook PDF)
    1. Insects—Juvenile literature. I. Title.
    QL467.2.M3647 2015
    595.7—dc23   2013050342

Editorial Credits
Nikki Bruno Clapper, editor; Cynthia Akiyoshi, designer; Kelly Garvin, media researcher;
Katy LaVigne, production specialist

Photo Credits
Dreamstime/Teresa Kenney, cover, back cover; Minden Pictures: Heidi & Hans Juergen Koch, 21, Kim Taylor, 9; Shutterstock: alexsvirid, 19, Bonnie Taylor Barry, 1, Lightboxx, 7, mchin, 13, smuay, 17, Souchon Yves, 11, Trofimov Denis, 5, Wasan Ritthawon, 15

Cover photo: grasshopper; title page photo: blue dasher dragonfly

Note to Parents and Teachers

The Animal Kingdom Questions and Answers set supports national curriculum standards for science related to the diversity of living things. This book describes and illustrates the characteristics of insects. The images support early readers in understanding the text. The repetition of words and phrases helps early readers learn new words. This book also introduces early readers to subject-specific vocabulary words, which are defined in the Glossary section. Early readers may need assistance to read some words and to use the Table of Contents, Glossary, Read More, Internet Sites, Critical Thinking Using the Common Core, and Index sections of the book.

Printed in the United States of America in North Mankato, Minnesota.
032014   008087CGF14

Table of Contents

Meet the Insects 4

Do Insects Have Backbones? 6

Are Insects Warm-Blooded or Cold-Blooded? 8

What Type of Body Covering Do Insects Have? 10

How Do Insects Eat? 12

Where Do Insects Live? 14

How Do Insects Have Young? 16

Do Insects Care for Their Young? 18

What Is a Cool Fact About Insects? 20

Glossary 22

Read More 23

Internet Sites 23

Critical Thinking Using the Common Core 24

Index 24

Meet the Insects

Buzz! A bee flies through the air.

Bees, ants, and butterflies are all insects.

These animals come in many shapes,

sizes, and colors.

bumblebee

Do Insects Have Backbones?

No, insects do not have backbones.

They do not have any bones at all.

Insects are invertebrates.

rhinoceros beetle

Are Insects Warm-Blooded or Cold-Blooded?

Insects are cold-blooded.

Their body temperatures go up

and down with their surroundings.

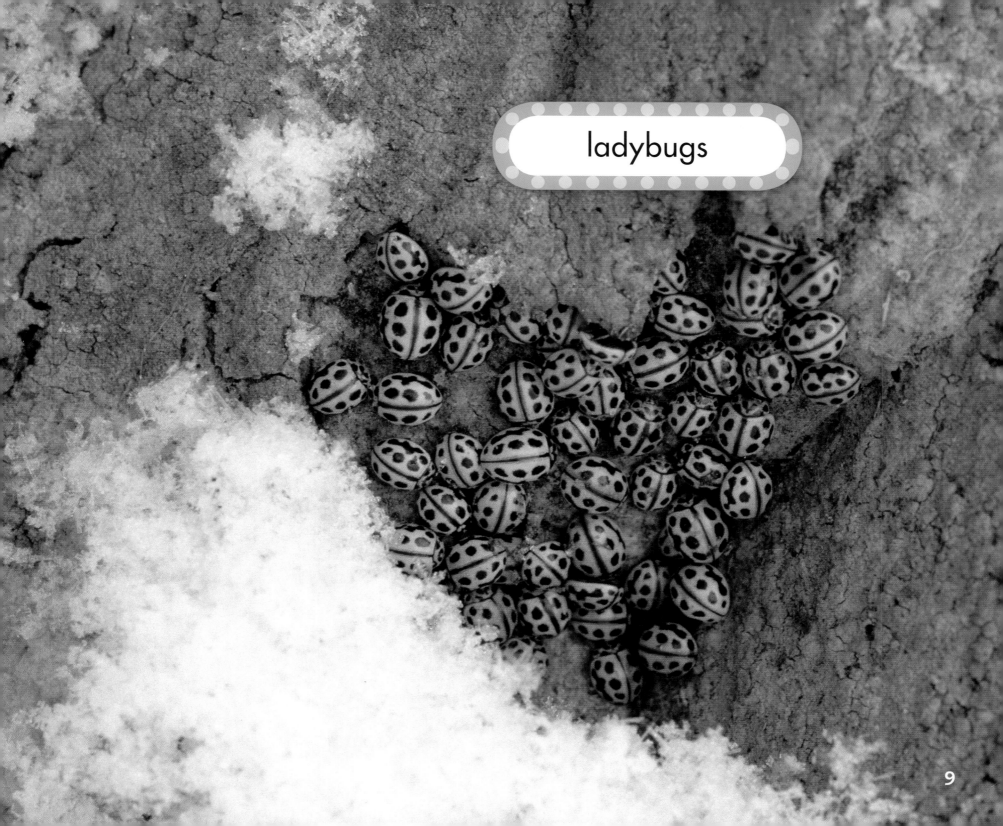

ladybugs

What Type of Body Covering Do Insects Have?

Insects have a hard skin covering

called an exoskeleton. Insects molt,

or shed their exoskeletons, as they grow.

All insects have six legs.

How Do Insects Eat?

Some insects eat plants.

Some insects eat other insects.

Most insects have strong jaws.

Their jaws move side to side.

grasshopper

Where Do Insects Live?

Insects live almost anywhere,
except really cold places
and oceans. Insects make
their homes in dirt, sand,
trees, and logs.

beetle

How Do Insects Have Young?

Some insects are born live.

Most hatch from eggs.

Many baby insects are called larvae.

They look like tiny worms.

mosquito babies

Do Insects Care for Their Young?

Most insects do not care for their young. But some insects live in groups. Wasps and bees feed and protect their young.

wasp nest

adult wasp

larvae

What Is a Cool Fact About Insects?

Honeybees and some other insects have tiny hairs all over their bodies. They even have hairs on their eyes.

hairs

honeybee

Glossary

cold-blooded—having a body temperature that changes with the surrounding temperature

exoskeleton—the hard outer shell of an insect; the exoskeleton covers and protects the insect

hatch—to break out of an egg

invertebrate—an animal without a backbone

larva—an insect at the stage of development between an egg and an adult; larvae means more than one larva

protect—to guard or keep safe from harm

temperature—the measure of how hot or cold something is

Read More

Hansen, Amy S. *Bugs and Bugsicles: Insects in the Winter*. Honesdale, Penn.: Boyds Mills Press, 2010.

Jenkins, Steve. *The Beetle Book*. Boston: Houghton Mifflin Books for Children, 2012.

Stewart, Melissa. *Zoom In on Grasshoppers*. Zoom In on Insects. Berkeley Heights, N.J.: Enslow Publishers, 2014.

Internet Sites

FactHound offers a safe, fun way to find Internet sites related to this book. All of the sites on FactHound have been researched by our staff.

Here's all you do:
Visit www.facthound.com
Type in this code: 9781491405642

Super-cool stuff! Check out projects, games and lots more at
www.capstonekids.com

Critical Thinking Using the Common Core

1. Insects have exoskeletons. What is an exoskeleton? (Craft and Structure)

2. Look at the pictures on pages 13 and 15. What do the bodies of insects have in common? (Integration of Knowledge and Ideas)

Index

ants, 4
babies, 16, 18
bees, 4, 18, 20
butterflies, 4
caring for young, 18
cold-blooded, 8
eating, 12, 18
eggs, 16
exoskeletons, 10

hairs, 20
invertebrates, 6
jaws, 12
larvae, 16
legs, 10
molting, 10
movement, 4
places to live, 14
wasps, 18

Word Count: 177
Grade: 1
Early-Intervention Level: 16